# OPERATION SQUIRREL

" Yes.".

Jesse shook a defiant fist whatsoever he evaluated prior to him. The. neighborhood was his for the snow fort was full. He had used 3 tall, slender birch trees as the edge posts for his lop-sided triangular domain of snow and also ice and also a few pieces of plywood hidden below the simulated snow stone front. Let's see Danny Fermburner kick that wall down with his dimension 10 boot or that huge high schooler who lives where Chubby made use of to live attempt to ride through it with his huge pee-yellow snowmobile. Jesse's grin curled almost as high as the Grinch's did prior to he moved down capital to dupe Whoville.

Jesse leapt to the front wall surface. He had actually developed his fort at the boundary edge of his backyard. Down the hill was the remainder of the sub-division. This snow covered mish-mash of plowed criss-crossing roads, snow-blown driveways and shoveled sidewalks, 2 of which he did for a dollar a piece, created an icy jungle of mounds and financial institutions and also drifts that would certainly become the.

sanctuaries and also burrows of the other youngsters that lived listed below.

" No one will get me," he said. He tilted back his head in Tarzan style to belt out a deafening scream of challenge that would certainly freeze all beasts listed below in worry.

As the first notes of his yawp attacked the ears of neighboring family pets, Ernie, Jesse's next door neighbor as well as good close friend shouted, "Hey Jesse.".

Jesse, astride the slippery wall, pivoted, panicked, as well as plummeted over the front and midway down capital, transforming his fearful cry into a sob of some neglected snow cow.

Chuckling, Ernie ran down after Jesse. Not being one of elegance and also strained with the mother-tested, kid-disapproved confusion of snow-gear that could increase as an area fit if it came with a helmet, Ernie stumbled over his dual protected, triple-socked foot. He detected the simply standing form of Jesse, and also they both grew out of control to the base of the hill.

" You klutz," claimed Jesse searching for into the skies.

Ernie raised his head. "Me, a lummox?" he stated. He punctuated capital. "Listen Ex-Lax, that's the one that did the smooth move up there.".

" I'll show you a smooth relocation." Jesse was up in a flurry of snow. "And currently the flying elbow drop." He resembled a step from Big-Time fumbling.

For the following couple of mins, the two children assaulted each other with bone squashing knee kicks, skull splintering head jams and rib splitting body pounds that reflected the same realistic look that was seen on TV consisting of commentators' narratives.

When both were winded, they laid in the run over ring of snow as well as watched as a couple of snows drifted down towards them.

Jesse grinned. "After this week, school's out 'til next year." He examined at Ernie to see if he captured the joke.

Ernie caught a snow with his tongue. "I'm not going to institution tomorrow.".

Jesse stayed up. "What?" He was eager to find any kind of solution that would eliminate any type of possibility of going to institution tomorrow or ever.

"Why?".

" Doctor.".

If he were taking medicine, Jesse made a face as. "Doctor, once more?" "Yep.".

" Hiiii-eeeee," said a voice from above.

Jesse as well as Ernie raised as well as admired see one of their worst concerns had actually come true. A girl remained in their fort. Not only that, it was Jesse's little sibling, Amanda, who had a track record of being the fastest tattle-tale in the sub- division. She might inform on somebody quicker than a sled on ice at Turner's Hill.

Jesse picked up a snowball and added capital. Amanda's head disappeared from the wall. Ernie dealt with Jesse, as well as the two of them listened to the pulling away cry of a specialist. "M-o-o-o-o-o-m-m-m-m-y-y-y!".

" Gees," said Jesse. "I didn't also do anything, as well as she's telling." "Well, at the very least you're not in trouble with the Telling Squirrel." Jesse took a look at Ernie. "Say what?".

" The Telling Squirrel," Ernie claimed. "I stopped you, as well as he didn't see.

you.".

" The who?".

" The Telling Squirrel." Ernie pointed to the top of among the trees that.

belonged of the ft. "See, right there.".

Jesse looked. A plump brownish squirrel leapt to a higher branch and entered into the nest that was there. Jesse looked back at Ernie and studied his face. Ernie was not a great liar, as well as by the expression on his face, Ernie looked dead major.

" What on the planet are you speaking about?".

Ernie stayed up. "That's the Telling Squirrel for the entire community." If he had actually made everything perfectly clear, he stopped with a nod of his head as.

" Yeah, so.".

Ernie rolled his eyes at his close friend's lack of expertise. "Look. As soon as in a while, Santa has this checklist that he inspects every. Every little thing you do is on the listing." Once again Ernie stopped.

Jesse thought for a minute attempting to assemble the two plus 2 that Ernie had actually provided him, but he still was not creating 4. "Go on," he said.

" How do you think Santa obtains all his details?".

Jesse paused prior to answering. "He just knows," he claimed. "Besides ...".

Ernie cut him off. "Grow up. Santa does not 'just knows.' He obtains all his info from the birds that fly back and forth from the North Pole. The squirrels watch everything and afterwards tell the birds, that fly up there and inform Santa." Ernie wiped his nose. "Its really quite simple.".

Jesse responded. Sure, it was fairly straightforward for a four year old, yet he was seven. So was Ernie. Santa is not real. Santa was ... well ... Jesse had actually not worked that part out.

" Santa's not real," he claimed as well as glimpsed as much as the tree were the squirrel's nest was to see if it had heard him. The squirrel was not there, as well as Jesse really felt eased. He did not desire the squirrel to hear what he had actually just said in instance Ernie's concept held true.

" He is also.".

" How do you recognize?".

" I understand," stated Ernie and in the world of 2nd graders, the statement 'I recognize' was proven reality.

Jesse responded to with the exact same step. "Well, I understand that he isn't," said.

Jesse.

Arrest. This meant there was just one respectable thing to do to.

settle the matter, and that was to obtain latest thing in.

" Is also.".

" Is not.".

" Is too.".

" Is not.".

According to all the 2nd quality codes, the disagreement would certainly need to continue until one of them batter the other up until he said 'uncle' or a higher power stepped in. The latter took place.

" J-e-e-s-s-e-e-e!" called Jesse's mom. "Dinner!".

And also prior to the resounding telephone call had actually ended up resounding off of the farthest home in the neighborhood, one more phone call intoned the evening from throughout the means. After that one more. Little numbers scurried from out of their exterior castles and play locations to rush home to the beckoning moms and dads. Jesse made note of where the Bartle doubles had actually come from, for the identical twins would be just one of his heaviest rivals during the snow battles to find.

Jesse and Ernie climbed up the hill and also strolled to their separate houses however not without an additional pair rounds of Is-Too-Is-Not. Right prior to going in, Jesse screamed his last "Is not," leapt within and also victoriously pounded the door.

Jesse addressed the phone after dinner. "Is too," claimed Ernie and hung up. Jesse hung up, and after that started to call Ernie. "What are you doing?" asked his mommy. "Nothing." Jesse hung up.

" Who was it?" she asked. "Ernie.".

" What did he want?" "Nothing.".

Jesse's mother grinned. "What are you 2 arguing around now.".

Gees, thought Jesse. In Between Amanda, Mom, and also the Telling Squirrel, he had not an opportunity.

" He's said there's a Santa Claus.".

" Oh," claimed his mother. She paused a moment to place the glasses in the sink. "Is there?".

" I do not believe so," he stated. "Why not?".

Jesse was not sure, so he used the typical parent evasion tool that he recognized ideal. "I do not understand.".

" Hmmm," claimed his mom, which was not the anticipated action. Jesse shuffled his feet. "Amanda said that you threw a snowball at her today.".

Mommy changed the topic. Jesse needed to assume fast. "Uh-uh," he stated. "I simply chased her a little.".

" Oh," she said. "Well, it's not wonderful to tease a person smaller than.

you.".

" Yes, ma'am.".

" You wouldn't want Santa to learn, would you?".

Jesse's heart missed a beat. Did Mom have the reduced down on the squirrel?

" He has ways of finding points out," she claimed.

She did. Santa had a spy network all worked out with squirrels as.

informants and birds as messengers. Why really did not any person inform me earlier?

" Let me assist with the dishes," he claimed quickly, as well as throughout the whole time, he maintained glimpsing out the window attempting to see if the squirrel might see him. Later that night, Jesse had a dream entailing a squirrel with a radio headset and field glasses.

Ernie was not in school Monday, neither was he in college all week. Jesse.

waited for him in the ft every mid-day, as well as whenever he mosted likely to the front door of Ernie's house, nobody was house. Jesse can not determine where Ernie was. By the end of the week, Jesse was stressed over Ernie and also himself. Two times the Bartle doubles had actually assaulted. The second time he also had Amanda help, yet she got hit in the face and told and also went Mom.

A couple of times Jesse had actually strolled know Mom and Dad that were speaking silently in their 'parent talk,' as well as he might have vowed they were discussing Ernie. It desired among these talks that they asked Jesse to take a seat.

" But I didn't do nothing," he claimed as he took a seat. It actually was not true, but he did not see the squirrel around either.

" Jesse," claimed Mom. "Ernie's is not well.".

" He's unwell." stated Dad. Mother offered an abuse appearance. Dad shrugged.

"What's incorrect with him?" asked Jesse.

" He has a severe condition with his blood," she said. "What do you indicate?".

" Well," she stopped briefly for a moment. "The blood is refraining its work in supplying the things he requires to the other components of his body.".

" Huh?".

" His blood doesn't work right," claimed Dad. "Oh.".

Once more Dad got the look. He shrugged.

" Anyway," she continued. "Ernie has to remain in the medical facility for awhile up until he gets better.".

" Oh, alright." Jesse responded his head. "Can I go see him?".

Jesse spoke before he assumed. Medical facilities had physicians that had medicine and also shots. Jesse shivered. His belly lifted and also down.

" Well, we'll see," said Mom. "It might be some time prior to he's well sufficient to see anyone.".

" Okay," said Jesse, a little bit relieved. "We can call him," said Dad.

" Great," said Jesse. Just connect and touch someone was better than existing at the health center.

Jesse complied with Dad to the kitchen phone as well as played with the lengthy phone cable while his Dad called Ernie's parents to consult them. They said it was alright and also provided Dad the area number.

" Hey Ernie, it's Jesse." "Jesse! Hi ya doin'?" "Good.".

" How was the recently of school?" Jesse rolled his eyes. "Long." "Yeah, I bet.".

Both fell quiet for a minute.

Jesse spoke out. "So what's happening with you?" "I'm unwell, dummy. That's why I'm in the health center.".

" Yeah, I know, you wimp. Do you desire me to get you a baby bottle?".

Ernie giggled, however after that at the other end, it seemed like he was practically crying. "Jesse, I'm scared.".

" Needles do that to me," said Jesse, not truly certain what to say. "I 'd rather do research than obtain a shot.".

Ernie laughed.

" So what ya' gettin' for Christmas?" asked Jesse. "Well, I ... Oh my gosh.".

" What?".

" Santa!".

" What concerning Santa?".

Ernie appeared anxious. "He won't involve the health center.".

Jesse first assumed was that he and Santa had something in common. "So, he'll leave his present at your house.".

" No, you do not comprehend. I got to talk to him. It's vital." "What do you suggest?".

" I reached ask him for something actually vital. It's the only method I'll improve.".

" What?".

" I can not inform you. It's my Christmas Wish. It's reached remain a secret.".

Jesse understood. Dreams had a far better opportunity of coming true if you maintained them a secret. Just like on birthday celebrations.

" Jesse?".

" Yeah.".

" You obtained' ta get me out of right here.".

Jesse's hand grasped the phone limited. Nurses with needles went through his mind. "What?".

" You got to get me out of right here for Christmas!".

For the following week, Jesse listened in on his moms and dads throughout their talks.

Ernie was actually ill. From what Jesse heard, Ernie could die if he did not have a special operation, but the medical professionals could not find what they were looking for to do the operation.

Jesse invested a great deal of time assuming concerning what Ernie had asked him to do: to breast him out of the hospital so he can chat to Santa Claus. Jesse despised healthcare facilities. And also, what if Santa Claus was unreal? What would he do after that? He couldn't let Ernie die; he was his best friend.

Jesse watched out at the ft. It was vacant. It was clear what he had to.

do.

He snuck to the phone as well as called Ernie.

" Hello.".

" This is agent K-28," stated Jesse. He decided that this secret procedure needed all precautions.

" This is Turtle Master," said Ernie.

Jesse always assumed that Ernie had a silly code name, yet he put it apart. "Be prepared," he stated. "Christmas Eve at Oh-Three-Hundred.".

" Roger.".

" Who's Roger?" said Jesse.

Ernie laughed. "I do not understand, however his last name is Wilco.".

Jesse chuckled and afterwards bore in mind something extremely crucial. "Hey, until now as well as Christmas Eve, you reached copulate the covers over your head.

If the registered nurse takes it off, you got to put it back on, alright. "Why?".

" Just do it." Jesse heard his mom turning up the stairways. "I obtained' ta go.".

Xmas Eve can be found in its common leisurely time for Jesse. It appeared that time slowed down increasingly more as the day came close to. Albert Einstein never even discussed this in his theory either. Time went the slowest in between the point were his parents said, "Its time for bed" and the actual point of going to sleep. In fact, right when he assumed he was falling asleep, he would certainly obtain delighted that he was dropping off to sleep as well as wake himself up. Tonight, nevertheless, Jesse could not also resemble going to sleep.

He had to obtain Ernie out of the medical facility. Jesse did attempt to, at the very least, unwind because it was mosting likely to take all his toughness to bring Ernie house.

Patiently, Jesse waited to hear his parents turn up the stairs to go to bed. With each other, Mom as well as Dad had come up the stairs twenty-four times but likewise had actually gone back down. Jesse rolled his eyes. Mama was always making him take points down to the cellar or upstairs by saying, "Save your self a trip later on.

and also take it up now with the various other things." That guideline did not appear to apply to his moms and dads tonite. Plus, Amanda woke up two times. When, for a beverage of water as well as once again to go to the restroom. Jesse translucented Amanda's spying tactics, for he had actually done it himself just 2 Christmas' ago. Do not parents ever track these points.

Ultimately, on the twenty-fifth flounder the stairs, Mom and Dad went to bed. Not without examining in on Amanda as well as then Jesse to see if they were asleep. As his parents opened his door, he transformed his head away and took deep, slow breaths to make it seem like he was sleeping.

" He's asleep," murmured Dad and also shut the door. Simply then, Jesse realized that he neglected to close his eyes. Because she would certainly have come in to kiss him good evening again, that would have been trouble if Mom checked on him.

Jesse stayed up in his bed. Last night it took his parents around a fifty percent an hour to go to sleep. This evening, Jesse waited forty minutes before relocating. After that, like a silent little fairy, he got clothed and also snuck downstairs. When he passed the living-room, the tinted lights from the Christmas Tree captured his eye. Jesse forgot to breath. It was attractive. The tree that was an odd-shaped uneven tree, was incredible. The lights shone merrily, showing off the rounds as well as accessories and also tinsel. The tree was marvelous like a bushy, big knight standing nobly over the plans as well as offers in its cost. The intense colored paper of the collection of presents mounded concerning the tree in its blocky salute to the vacation. At the very base of the tower of pine and paper was Mom's nativity collection. Father had actually made the stable from scrap pieces of wood, and also it was the only present he was able to provide her their very first Christmas together. The figurines, which were handed down to her from her granny, that had actually looked used and also chipped when Mom set them up, now looked to life in the shimmering lights. Whatever shimmered joyously. Jesse wiped a tear from his eyes as well as rushed to the basement to put on.

his snow equipment, pack a layer and boots for Ernie as well as get his sled. He did not even see the HO train established with mountain passage as well as canyon that he had wanted a lot because the Christmas brochure came in very early September. He was half way down the street before he realized that he was still smiling. His heart was battering, as well as he felt like he could run all the way to the hospital.

When he ran out variety of the last streetlight toward the dark end of the street, he stopped briefly. Everything looked scary. The tree by the roadway looked bigger against the moon with its branches cutting black lines right into its face making it appear like a big broken plate. Absolutely nothing moved. Jesse checked out the vacant lot and at the route that cut diagonally across to the main road. In the summer, they took the trail to the pop store to buy candy. After that it would certainly be down the road, across the railway tracks and to the left. Jesse jumped over the shallow ditch as well as on to the trail. It had been flattened by a snow sled. His red sled with yellow manages hissed behind as well as periodically faced the rear of his boots. Above him the stars sparkled like frost overhead. The snow crunched under his boots. Steam rippled from his nose and also mouth. Jesse thought about a train and also began to run. He blew out his breath like an engine, as well as prior to he understood it, he was throughout the area at the edge of somebody's yard. Considering that he was working on the snow sled track, he had veered of the trail without recognizing it. Down better he can see the top of the pop store's sign. Jesse set off towards the shop.

The snowmobile trail went around the side of the shed. There, parked by the much side of the shed was a black snowmobile. It did not look like the filthy yellow one that high schooler drove. Jesse treked on through a deep drift. He recalled over his shoulder. The snowmobile glimmered in the moonlight. He stopped. He can obtain Ernie conveniently with it. Would not it be taking? Jesse recognized he would certainly return it, but still, should he? Jesse backtracked toward the snow sled.

He touched the handlebar.

" No, I 'd better not," he claimed. "Besides, I could not even start it.".

Jesse's heart skipped a beat. There, in the console, in the ignition that reviewed 'electric beginning' was a secret. He dropped his sled as well as was about to hop on when he discovered squirrel tracks in the snow on the seat. Momentarily Jesse hesitated, however he promptly cleaned the snow from the seat and also sat down. He 'd clarify it to Santa after Ernie told his Christmas Wish. Jesse can hardly see over the dash by sitting, so he knelt on the seat. Swiftly, he grabbed the essential and also twisted. The snowmobile thrummed to life, as well as Jesse was off. Off the seat and in the snow. He had squeezed the throttle to quick, as well as it lurched from below him. Jesse raised as well as back on the delayed machine. No lights began.

Once again Jesse started it, and thoroughly, he drove away from your home. He only fell off again prior to reaching the hospital.

The lift doors glided open with a stifled 'bung,' and also Jesse scampered throughout the tiny hall and also behind a plant. The 'bung' had actually frightened him half to fatality, so he sat behind the plant for a full five mins attempting to bear in mind exactly how to breath normally. Jesse didn't recall James Bond ever having problems breathing.

Jesse saw a registered nurse come out of an office behind the big counter of the nurses' terminal. Above the counter was an indication with arrowheads as well as area numbers. Ernie's area was to the right. Quietly, Jesse laid down the coat as well as boots for Ernie and his own boots that he had actually removed in the elevator. They had actually clumped as well loud in the hall downstairs.

Something behind the counter went 'bing,' and the nurse looked over at the panel as well as then went down the hall to the. Jesse went to the edge as well as saw the nurse decrease one more hallway. Jesse sprinted to Ernie's area.

" Ernie?".

The room was dark except for the light from the window.

Ernie turned up from a mound of coverings from the closest bed. "Jesse?" he stated.

" Let's go."

Jesse went over to the bed as well as aided Ernie go out. Jesse arranged the cushions in a row and covered it with a covering. "See," he said. "It looks like you're still right here."

" I've been sleeping with the covers over my head ever since you informed me," stated Ernie with a grin. "And the registered nurses stopped pulling them off just a number of days back."

Jesse responded. "Now they'll never ever understand you're gone."

Both boys mosted likely to the door and peered out. The nurse was returning. They pulled back behind the door.

" Now what?" asked Ernie.

Jesse swung Ernie to be still. "When she goes by, we run in the direction of the elevators. Our stuff is behind a plant. We take the stairs down." Jesse did not wish to await a lift or another 'bung'.

The registered nurse passed, Jesse counted to 5, and they bolted out the door, skittering on their equipping feet.

When the nurse got to the last space, she located a little woman out cold with her hand snuggling the call button. The registered nurse tucked her in with a smile and returned to her terminal without understanding that a person had actually snuck out.

It was close 5 in the morning. Jesse and also Ernie had slept in a slouched pile on top of one another on the couch in Ernie's living-room. Jesse mixed and gradually stayed up. Ernie's head went down to Jesse's leg. Jesse pulled the knitted afghan off the back of the couch as well as spread it out with an uncomfortable toss over Ernie's small huddled body.

Jesse looked over Ernie's tree that was simply at the end of the sofa. It was a great tree wonderfully decorated with many handmade crafts and ornaments. There were just a few presents under the tree. The majority of were to Ernie. In fact, Jesse, from were he was sitting, can just construct out two awkwardly wrapped presents that were for Ernie's mother and father. The one-of-a-kind style of covering which made use of a great deal of tape and uncertain folds suggested that they were wrapped with the really real treatment of Ernie's fingers. Jesse could not grin however assist.

Jesse was beginning to dosage off, so when Santa stepped out from the opposite side of the tree, Jesse didn't even flinch. He looked large to Jesse in his white cut red match. The black natural leather of his belt as well as boots caught all the shades of light from the tree in shining brilliance. His round bearded face wrinkled with a smile and beamed with mirth. His eyes sparkled like the stars that Jesse had actually seen previously tonite.

" Whew, I was obtaining a little anxious," Jesse said in a rather informal manner that stunned himself. Inside, his heart, mind, and soul thrummed with exhilaration, yet gradually, like hot delicious chocolate heating him up from the inside, he stired up. "Santa!" he whispered, bearing in mind not to wake Ernie's parents.

Santa chuckled. "Merry Christmas, Jesse." He tipped closer. "What a delighted child," he said as he bent down to take a look at Ernie's face. "You're a buddy, Jesse." If to go, he stood up as well as transformed as.

" Santa," stated Jesse. "Ernie's got a Christmas Wish he's got to tell you."

Once more he chuckled in that wonderful voice of his. "It's currently been approved. You have seen to that."

" I did?"

" Sure. Ernie just wished to be house for Christmas." "But, he's actually unwell," claimed Jesse.

" Yes," claimed Santa with a depressing smile. "He is."

" Can't you make him better."

" That I can refrain. I can just give as well as urge others to provide." "Who can aid him?"

Santa considered the nativity established on the piano. "Who else?" Santa smiled. "He obtained me started."

" Got you began in what?" "Giving.".

" Giving?".

" Yes, offering to others," said Santa. "And you have offered Ernie the most

significant present anybody could ever before provide anyone else: himself." Santa frowned. "Or herself." Santa laughed. "Let's simply claim 'the giving of oneself'.".
" Jesus informed you to do that?" "No. He revealed me." "Huh?".
Santa grinned an elfish smile. "You'll figure it out," he said. "Anyway, what is your Christmas Wish?".
Jesse believed for a moment. He looked at Ernie's round, glowing face. "I simply want Ernie to be better.".
Santa leaned near to Jesse's face. His eyes glowed even brighter. "You have that gift in you already.".
Santa went back as well as drew a big cream color pipeline from his pocket. He placed it to his mouth and also lit it. He blew a large smoke ring that drifted over his cap like a halo. The ring grew to the size of a hula-hoop. "Don't fret about the snowmobile," he winked and also claimed. The smoke ring went down to the floor, as well as Santa was gone.
Jesse looked at the dissipating smoke ring with surprise. That squirrel was quicker than Jesse thought. Jesse leaned back and also closed his eyes and also went to sleep.

Jesse woke up in a blur of concerns from Ernie's mom and dad, his mom and dad, Amanda, and two policemen.
" I was mosting likely to return it, honest," said Jesse out of reflex. The area fell quiet. "What?" said one of the police officers. "Uh ... nothing," claimed Jesse.
Jesse's mama sat down beside him. "Honey," she claimed. "Why 'd you do. it?".
Jesse blinked. Suddenly it appeared he dreamed the whole thing,.
including sneaking Ernie out of the hospital. Jesse looked concerning for Ernie, yet did not see him. "Where's Ernie?".
" We believed you fled," claimed Dad. "Until Ernie's moms and dads called and also said you were asleep on their couch.".
" How would certainly you get in?" asked the various other officer. "Where's Ernie?" said Jesse, a little louder.
" Why did you come over here?" asked Ernie's mother. Jesse yelled, "Where's Ernie?".
Everyone gazed and froze at Jesse. "He's at the hospital," said his.

mother.

" No, I'm not." All wanted to see a sleepy-faced Ernie standing in the. center of the staircases scrubing his eyes.

" Ernie!" shouted Jesse's and also Ernie's parents.

Ernie's mommy ran up the stairs with his papa close behind. She grabbed him and also embraced him. "Ernie, for God's benefit, what are you doing home?".

" I wanted to be home for Christmas," stated Ernie, starting to sob. "I'm. sorry.".

Ernie's mother hugged Ernie. "It's alright, child. I'm grateful you're below," she. claimed. Tears ran down her cheeks.

" How would certainly you get here?" asked Ernie's daddy. Amanda spoke up. "Jesse did it.".

" Be quiet, Amanda," said Jesse's mama.

Alright, some justice, believed Jesse. Mama hugged Jesse closer, as well as he discovered she was crying, also.

" It's alright, Mom," claimed Jesse. "Santa said I have the ideal kind of bone marrow that Ernie needs." Jesse's mother checked out him with surprise, however her face did not contain as much shock as Jesse's own face. He did not keep in mind Santa stating that, however he knew it was proper.

When Jesse awoke in the medical facility bed, it was two months later. Ernie was in the bed next to him, and everyone was there. Whatever was blurred. The light from the window beyond of Ernie made his eyes injured. Jesse heard a doctor saying that is was incredible just how the two kids matched perfectly for the procedure, and also they just lived a house a part, which the operation and also transfer worked out. Jesse saw Ernie smile at him.

" Is too," stated Ernie, hardly above a murmur.

Jesse grinned. Outside on the window walk, a squirrel scuttled by.

# THE LAST MINUTE GIFT

From his vantage point on top of the large stairs in front of Thomas's Department Store, Joe checked the river of Christmas shoppers. It was a tumultuous river with ebbs, currents and also savage undertows. He had seen produced males and females pulled down, clutching their packages like life preservers, just to be washed up on an island of benches where others have actually been abandoned by the real hunters, or on the shore of the shopping center gallery where people of teenagers collected. Yes, it was a river of layers, bags and humankind. It was the Christmas Eve thrill, getting eleventh hour gifts. Joe sighed. His layer hung heavily on his sagging shoulders. Weight pushed down on him. It had been a lengthy year when the lay-off came. It caused a new task in a brand-new community away from households. No problem ... Life's a roller coaster. Today, here, currently, Joe found more things pushing in on him. The automobile's transmission, the second job to pay for the extra expenses and the maternity his wife.

just uncovered. All this was seasoned with his boy's recent struggles with high temperatures, coughs and ear infections.
Joe felt his appropriate shoulder droop as if it was being drawn to the flooring.
"Hey!" Joe wrenched his shoulder up as well as glared at the small young boy

who.
had actually been pulling on his layer. His temper quickly vanished.
" I appeared to have been divided from my mommy," stated the little kid.
Joe looked at him. The child looked regarding 5 or 6. He had curly dark hair and also brilliant brownish eyes. His face was round and also fragile with blushing cheeks. Joe crouched down, allowing the bags he was carrying remain on the floor.
" Excuse me," he claimed.
The young boy mixed his feet. "I appeared to have been separated from my. mommy.".
Joe chuckled. The kid's option of words amused him despite the fact that the. child was lost.
" Well," stated Joe. "We'll need to fix that circumstance." "That would be good," stated the boy.
Joe studied the kid more carefully. He had eyes that seemed mild as well as clear. He felt unwinded. "Where is your mother?".
" She is at the mall." The young boy's eyes were vast with innocence.
Joe laughed. "Okay, we'll most likely to the shopping center protection office."
The young boy nodded in contract. "What's your name?" asked Joe.
" I'm not supposed to offer my name to complete strangers," he claimed. "I see," said Joe.
" What's yours?" said the boy. "Joe".
" Is that your first name?".
Joe frowned at the inquiry. "No, really it's my middle name because my papa has the same first name as well as ..." Joe stopped. He discovered it odd to be.

clarifying this to the little child in the center of the mall. "Look, I require to obtain home, so allow's go.".
" Okay.".
Joe stood with a groan, his exhausted bones creaking. Next, he got his bags, adjusted one under his arm and also extended his hand to the young boy.
" Ready?" asked Joe.
" Ready." The child grabbed onto Joe's hand firmly.
Joe looked back to the river and fell to the flow of deal seekers, bringers of joy as well as procrastinators. He caught a great present moving in the instructions

he wanted to go up until a male swam upstream like a salmon as well as crashed right into them, tipping on the young boy's foot.
" Ouch!".
" Sorry," stated the individual and also swam on. "You okay?" asked Joe.
" He injured my foot." The young boy stood on one leg.
People scrambled into them knocking the young boy into Joe's leg. Joe rapidly scooped the young boy up with his appropriate arm. He jumped the child on his hip to get a far better hold and then carried on.
Sweat dripped under his garments, and his arms moaned with the weight of the packages and the child. A muscle mass spasm surged in his arm, and he moaned. Looking around, he spied a collection of benches by a treat cart. Joe floundered via a college of travelling kids and set the child on the bench.
He rolled his arm around to relax his shoulder.
" Looks as if we are mosting likely to have to make a modification," he stated. Joe set the bags he was carrying on the bench. "Come here," stated Joe as he grabbed the little child and also swung him around onto his back. Joe dipped down. "Okay, climb up on my shoulders." The young boy followed his directions. Joe gradually cleaned, examining the weight on his back. The kid felt as weightless.

" Good," stated Joe as he ordered his bags by the manages. The two little bags went into his right, the large one in his. "That must do it.".
The child patted Joe's head. "We're doing fine," he said.
Joe chuckled as well as waded back into the flow of the Christmas rush.
The going was very easy initially, but the handles of the bags started to attack right into his hands. The child no more appeared light. And, every bump from one more consumer felt like hitting a rock. The prickling warm scrubed underneath his layer, and also his legs felt as if he were actually moving with warm, sloppy water.
The boy became larger. Joe's back scrunched under the weight however stayed firm. He had actually figured that the boy considered more than his very own son, for his kid was 4, yet he might not believe how hefty the child had ended up being in the last few minutes. Joe started desiring that the mom would detect her child on his shoulders. He asked yourself where she was.
Joe remembered the determined fifteen mins he had when he lost his boy in

2014. His heart fluttered with the remembrance of that day. He had actually been frightened. He remembered running through the shop screaming as images of the scaries of what could take place to lost kids blinked with his mind.
Joe steeled himself as well as treked on. The kid on his shoulders had been lucky that he had located Joe, that's without a doubt. Joe also grabbed his pace. He did not like the suggestion of a stressed mom.
A bag ripped open as well as splashed the two wrapped presents on the floor. Joe vowed. He spun around trying to locate packages.
" Here mister," stated a woman pushing packages under his arm. "Thanks," he claimed. He clamped his elbow versus them. "That's actually.

good ..." tale.".

" Yeah, yeah," she swirled away. "I do not have time for a Christmas Joe went back to his mission. "Okay," he claimed. "We're nearly there.".

The boy patted Joe's head once again. "You can do it.".
Joe ground on. His arms ached. The boxes under his arm slipped sometimes, and he pressed his arm tighter against them. The child seemed like a lead weight gradually grinding right into his shoulder blades. Sweat trickled right into his eyes stinging his vision.
' Mall Security' check out an indication directing down a narrow hall.
Joe stepped out of the chaos of people as well as mixed down the hall. "Almost there," claimed the young boy.
The last few lawns, his back burned and also his shoulders yelled, but his legs remained steady.
With a groan, Joe dipped his shoulders, as well as the kid clambered onto the high counter. Joe established the bags on the floor and also gradually drew the boxes out from under his arm and set them on the counter.
" How can I assist you?" stated the guard. "This kid's shed.".
" What's your name, child?" stated the guard. The child smiled and told him.
Joe checked out the young boy. "You told him your name, but you wouldn't tell.

me.".

The youngster's eyes sparkled. "You're not a law enforcement officer." Joe moaned and placed his head down on the counter.
The boy patted Joe's shoulder. "Christopher," claimed the boy. Joe looked.

up. "I recognize that's your given name.".
Joe straightened, his eyes secured on the little kid's face. There was a radiance about him.
" Christopher," claimed the young boy. "I understand the globe has actually been heavy upon you but do not stress. You are solid." The kid gently put his hand on Joe's cheek. "You have carried me and also have actually felt the full weight. Your confidence will constantly.

keep you strong, now and at the following river." The young boy's eyes were not of a little boy, yet of a kind and caring and caring being, which drew him right into a heat. "Go in tranquility.".
" Christopher!" Joe turned to see that called, as well as the young boy was gone.

The next morning, Joe located himself cuddled up on his sofa with his spouse and also his child. His child's fever was gone. They were all just cuddling with each other after an attractive morning of Christmas joy.
Joe's shoulder ached, and also he groaned as well as stretched. His kid reached up and touched his cheek. Again, Joe really felt the warmth he felt the day previously. His kid scrubed the tear away from his check and also smiled.

# THE FIRST KNIGHT OF CHRISTMAS

The peasant vacation of this land appeared, to Sir Michael, one of malarkey. For certain, a lowly youngster born in a steady. or manger ... or drop gave little reason to commemorate. However as a part of the knight's code that was advised to him when he was a squire and also prior to his mission stated, "Do not ridicule others, the uneducated deserve training, not reject.".

With that idea, Sir Michael pushed his huge war-horse onward right into the bitter wind toward the village. From the hovel that caught his interest with beautiful lights and petition, a hymn emerged that seemed most joyous. He was in a dour state of mind. His pursuit was now involving the close of its third cycle through the seasons, as well as he had yet to find what he was stated to locate: "Worth of one's life.".

All knights of the king were sent on this mission, as well as all knights returned asserting their well worth. A lot of said that they have saved a kid, secured the meek, defended the inadequate or enjoyed a flower bloom. Sir Michael, himself, had actually done these deeds many layer, also the watching of a blossom. Yet, he did not feel he had asserted his very own well worth. Due to the fact that he would certainly obtain burnt out and miss the blossoming or his equine would certainly consume the bud, as well as the flower seeing took 2 weeks.

His mind rattled on back to sporadic minutes of his training. "Worth is.

not always determined by the activity however by the one that is doing the action." That phrase haunted the knight after every achievement. Also after he had conserved a village from a band of burglars and also was commemorated by the town for two days, he did not feel he was of well worth.

His horse stopped at the gatepost of the inn. , Sir Michael dismounted and also with the hefty actions of shield, knocked upon the door. It opened up with a blaze of light.

" There's no more area ..." stated the Innkeeper, yet when he saw the tall knight with the light of the inn shining off his plate mail and hilt of his sword, he rapidly bowed. "I'm sorry, sir knight. My humble inn is crowded, but I'm certain I can discover you a bed. I 'd be recognized to include a worthy knight.".

" Thank you, my great man," stated Sir Michael. "I will stable my horse as well as remain in for a little while.".

" My boy can take care of your horse," stated the innkeeper.

" Thy offer is most kind, nevertheless, a knight of the world have to personally attend to his equine." Sir Michael then estimated a flow from training. "' The horse that serves a knight well, must be offered well by the knight.' Therefore, my equine deserves my treatment.".

The innkeeper responded pleasantly. "I will find you some food." He quickly closed the door to quit the chill of the night leaving Sir Michael in the icy darkness.

The wind gusted as Sir Michael opened up the stable door, and it tore from his hand. The door slammed versus the external wall with a mighty collision, as well as horse and knight unwittingly rushed right into the dark shelter of a much earlier time after that whence they were from.

When inside, Sir Michael muscled the door versus the wind, as well as it.

banged closed. Turning about and also progression to evaluate the accommodations for his horse, he encountered the small frame of a male who stood warily, yet frankly in front of the knight with his work-worn hands on a personnel that was thrust defensively onward.

As his eyes gotten used to the dim light, Sir Michael can see that because straw behind the man was a female holding a babe. They were nestled into a pet stall. Their burro was silently chewing to their side. There was an open pack showing clothing, woodworker's tools as well as a handmade toy of timber. The simple woodworker did not alter his strong position.

Michael researched the guy's eyes. The dark brownish eyes showed much to the knight; he checked out that the guy had identified the size, the toughness, as well as the sword of his. There was a trembling of worry blended with the assurance of love, prepared to protect his household. Behind the spouse, the mommy turned her shoulder as if to secure the youngster. Her eyes were wide with a mix of unpredictability as well as defiance. The knight recognized that this small guy was ready to combat; all set to eliminate versus great chances to shield his child. He read the same from the mom's company shoulders. Prior to the knight were 2 frightened moms and dads, yet he might feel love, strength and also guts.

Sir Michael held his hand up and after that silently relied on tend to his.

horse.

While he unbridled, fed, as well as combed his place, Sir Michael watched the little family members. The husband knelt by his better half as well as babe during unless he stepped away to explore, eyes broad with problem, the noises from the winter season storm outside. Also after that he would never go more than two paces from his family members. He would go back to them promptly as well as draw the covering more securely around his spouse's shoulder and tuck the little chubby hand of the infant back under the folds up. Minutes later, the hand would squirm totally free again, as well as the.

daddy would grin, and his eyes would certainly crinkle in mirth before he patiently and carefully assisted the small hand back beneath the wool. The mother would grin and kiss his cheek.

The tiny side door of the shed banged open. The daddy sprang to his feet, staff at the ready. Wind cut into the area and also little bit against the cheeks of Sir Michael. In stepped two shabbily dressed guys. Hoods hid their faces. They looked upon the tiny dad as well as responded, not seeing Sir Michael behind the big steed.

The unfamiliar people shut the door as well as advance as their hands reached underneath their torn cloaks. The papa tighten his hold on his personnel. All, nonetheless, iced up. A cold-blooded hiss of Sir Michael's enormous sword arising from its scabbard sent out chills around the stable. Its sharp blade reeled in the light, catching it on its edge as well as glowing. Sir Michael stepped to the carpenter's side.

Both complete strangers ingested and gradually extracted a loaf of bread, cheese, and a tinder box. Meticulously they progression and also laid this at the dad's feet.

When the door turned open again throughout that icy night, 3 richly clothed males actioned in to discover a tiny fire thoroughly ringed by rocks in front of a family members. The spouse knelt easily beside his spouse's shoulder as they both look admirably upon their youngster. The kid was healthy and balanced with red cheeks and energetic hands that played in the flickering light. Away were two guards professionally viewing and also appreciating the family members. And also to the other side, towered a knight in dazzling steel. His two big gauntleted hands rested on the pommel of his sword that stood like a cross before him. The papa searched for briefly to note who had actually come in, responded appreciatively, after that returned his look to his boy. His eyes were certain, delighted, and loosened up. The mom's face was calm as well as smooth and also glowing.

The kings bowed. The child did be entitled to the protection of somebody mighty. Silently, they laid prior to the family gold, incense as well as myrrh. As well as they also, withdrawed a considerate distance and admired the babe.

Sir Michael stood attentive the whole evening as others saw to pay their regard to the humble family members. If he was anticipated to be there, no one appeared to questions the knight's existence; it was as.

His muscular tissues never ever tired as the family members snuggled into each others arms as well as went to rest. And also the papa and mother rested well, for although they kept in their arms the greatest power understood to male, they were but human, as a result needed peace of mind of a questing knight standing calmly off to the side.

In the morning, the daddy stepped prior to Sir Michael, and they squeezed hands as those who safeguard do. After that the gentle mother stepped forward as well as touched Sir Michael's cheek. He considered her face; gratefulness emitted forth from her kind, soft eyes.

She held the infant towards Sir Michael. The terrific knight knelt as well as was still able to look upon the child's face. Sir Michael realized that he had actually been the ignorant which he had actually been taught. His quest mored than, his well worth had actually been found from within while securing a small, frightened carpenter's household on a cold wintertime night.

Sir Michael, the mighty guy he was, then laid his sword on the ground prior to the infant; a motion of vouched loyalty. A little tender hand got to forward as well as deliberately touched his ideal shoulder, then his left, then the knight's temple.

Thus, Sir Michael had been dubbed First Knight by the King of Kings.27

# GOOD STUFF

Ringlets of brown curls bounced frantically with every dive of Heidi Louise's temper tantrum.

" I don't want an infant for Christmas! I don't desire an infant for Christmas."

Her tirade would certainly have been much more reliable if she had not been on her bed, yet she really did not want her moms and dads to hear. It was likewise the reason she really had not been screaming however wearing out a loud whisper. She had actually also pulled her drapes and also shut her door. Any type of witnesses would certainly have been damaging to what was left of the opportunity of a great Christmas. No bad reports required to return to Santa.

Her dives shed effectiveness, and her throat was starting to hurt from her "silent" shouting. She plunked on her bed.

" Now, don't you feel better," claimed Julie. Her brown eyes big and caring. Heidi cleared her throat. "I guess."

Julie climbed up on to the bed. Being that she was eight, an entire 2 years older then Heidi, Julie was the expert on all problems. Specifically on problems of having younger brothers as well as sisters. Likewise, she was able to enjoy talk shows and also was mosting likely to be a "cycle-thera-piss" when she was twelve.

When Julie had to do with

to reveal some great trick that was televised to the masses, she would say, "As Dr. Joan would certainly state ..." Every little bit of recommendations came from Dr. Joan, a name that stuck to her from an episode of Rosie.

" As Dr. Joan would claim," Julie's temple furrowed with deep concentration, "it is important to release your emotions, so they venture out."

" Huh?" Heidi did not constantly understand the pearls of knowledge that Julie passed on yet knew deep down that Julie was right.

Julie rolled her eyes. "If they stay in, you might get a tumor." If she cleared it all up, Julie held her hand out hands up as.

" A lump?"

" Yeah.".

" Oh." Heidi claimed to understand. Occasionally, with Julie, it was best to act. Heidi altered the topic.

" Do you assume any individual saw or listened to?" "No." Julie trembled her head.

Heidi sighed. "I do not want to get in any kind of trouble. It's so near to Christmas, as well as I wan' na get ...".

Julie covered her mouth as well as completed Heidi's sentence "... good things." Julie's eyes were substantial. "Don't ever before state a desire aloud. It could make it go away.".

Heidi responded, happy for her cousin's caution. She stopped briefly and then asked, "Is it truly negative to have an infant?".

" Yes," claimed Julie. "They poop over everything." She made a face. "It truly stinks as well. Brian was constantly throwing up. He threw up on me two times.".

" Yuck," said Heidi.

" One time, his diaper came off, as well as he was going through the house, and also mom was attempting to capture him. He ran right into my room and also peed on my dolls. They each cost $500 dollars at Super-Mart." Heidi recognized that every little thing.

Julie had actually cost $500. "I needed to toss them away.".
An expression of fear tipped over Heidi face. "Plus, they take your things as well as never give it back.".
Heidi eyed her packed canine, Waldo. "No one will certainly get you." "Uh-huh," Julie stated.
Heidi grabbed her brownish packed dog and also began to weep.

" Mommy?".
" Yes, dear.".
" Can you read me Clifford?" Julie had actually gone house a couple of hrs back, and also the effects of her counseling were haunting Heidi.
" Sure." Mom patted the cushion close to her. Heidi started to climb up onto her mommy's lap.
" No, dear. I don't have area for you in my lap. I'm also large.".
Heidi pouted a bit as well as sighed, however she unwillingly sat beside her mom. She crossed her arms, but she actually didn't listen. The infant had not been even right here, and it was hindering currently. Julie was right. They take your stuff as well as never give it back.

Santa still looked a little bit scary, yet Heidi had some crucial concerns to discuss with him.
" Can I speak with him alone," she stated. Father overlooked. "What, honey? "I'm

a large lady. I can do it myself.".

Father smiled. "Okay, I'm certain you can." Heidi assumed he appeared a little unfortunate. "I'll stand over below.".

Heidi marched deliberately approximately Santa and also was swooped up by a really high fairy and plopped onto his legs. Santa's bearded face was unexpectedly really close.

" Ho-ho-ho," said Santa. "What's your name?" "Heidi Louise," she whispered.

" What a pretty name." Heidi responded.

" Have you been great?".

Santa's beard itched her cheek, and also he smelled like pepper mint. Heidi responded once more.

" What would certainly like for Christmas?".

All the toys she had attracted circle in the Christmas brochure disappeared from her thoughts. She shrugged.

" How around a little doll-ie," stated Santa. "A child ..." "No," stated Heidi swiftly. "Not an infant. No children." Santa blinked and also wrinkled his eyebrows. "What?" "I simply want mom as well as daddy and also me.".

Santa's voice appeared to transform. "I do not think ..." Heidi released out of Santa's lap and also went to her Daddy. "All set," Daddy claimed.

Heidi tried as well as responded to smile.

Heidi saw an ambulance at her residence when they were driving down the road to their home. Daddy stayed up straighter in his seat as well as claimed a word that was not intend to be stated. The automobile quickened.

Heidi was discouraged.

The auto jerked, and Daddy was leaping out of the vehicle. "Stay in there," he stated. She craned her neck and watched him run up the drive. Two guys were lugging Mommy on a cot. Dad's arms were swing and afterwards getting to help carry her.

Heidi was laying awake. Downstairs she listened to the phone ring, as well as she hid under her covers. Something was incorrect. Dad had actually selected Mommy in the ambulance, and Heidi needed to stay at the next-door neighbors until her Grampa Glade turned up.

For the remainder of the evening, he had actually simply grinned at her as well as colored as well as played. Whenever the phone rang, he would go in the kitchen to address it. He would say "yep" and also "fine" a whole lot, which really did not assist Heidi figure out that he was speaking with or about. He would certainly complete every call with an "Everything is going to be great." Then Grampa would come back as well as smile as well as ask her about Santa or what she wanted for Christmas. She would certainly tell him about the playthings but not what she informed Santa at the shopping mall.

She raised her bed covers. He was still on the phone.

Heidi slid out of bed and also went to her door. The hall light was on, however she might get near the stairways and also still stay hidden.

" Yep," claimed Grampa Glade.

Heidi rolled her eyes. Doesn't he ever state anything on the phone, she assumed.

"That's good," he claimed. "And Louise?".

Heidi got hold of the railing. They were talking about Mommy. Heidi's middle name coincided as her mommy's.

" Oh," he stated.

A cool rose her back. It didn't seem great.

" Okay, after that." Grampa Glade removed his throat. "Everything's mosting likely to be great." He hung up the phone.

She began to cry. What had she done? She shouldn't have actually informed Santa anything.

" Heidi Louise," stated Grampa Glade as he showed up the staircases. "It's my fault," said Heidi.

He picked her up. "Child," he said. "That's nonsense." He brought her to her space.

Heidi sobbed as well as informed him concerning her wish with Santa. He paid attention and held her for a very long time. He talked when she had stopped crying.

" There was an additional infant, a long time ago that no one wanted." "Not also the moms and dads?".

" Oh, the moms and dads wanted him quite. Not as well several other individuals did. There had not been even space at the motel. He was born in a barn.".

Heidi transformed her head up. "It sounds like Jesus.".

Grampa Glade smiled. When her grampa grinned, his eyes would certainly glimmer, and he would look like a fairy. "You are so clever." He embraced her close.

" You see," he said. "Some individuals hesitated of infant Jesus due to the fact that he was mosting likely to alter whatever. So, they attempted to stop him from pertaining to the world. It was just that they didn't understand that he was bringing good ideas.".

" Is Mommy's infant bringing good ideas." "You bet' cha.".

" Julie says that infants bring poop.".

He laughed. "Yes, they do bring poop." "And she said they bring 'hyper-steria'."

"Julie sees excessive television.".

" Then what do babies bring?

" Good things," he stated. "Babies bring joy as well as happiness. Babies bring soft blurry clothing as well as make adults go 'goo-goo gah-gah.' He tickled her, and she chuckled. "Babies bring burps and laughs. Babies bring individuals to love and also care about.".

" What else do they bring.".

Grampa Glade smiled, and also his eyes were watery. "You. They bring you." He held her close. "How do you think I obtained you?".

Heidi felt warm and safe. "I like being hugged."

"Babies do too," he said. "And they need a lot of hugging."

"From their mommies?"

"Yes. Especially their mommies. And their daddies."

"Do they need more then big kids?"

He pulled back and looked at her. "Yes, in a way they do."

Heidi sighed, "Oh."

"But," he said. "Big kids get something more."

"What?"

"To be a big brother or sister. They get to hold babies and play with them and protect them. This is a very special job. Mommies and Daddies give this job only to the oldest. It makes the big kid important."

"Im-portant? What does it mean?"

"It means that you are really loved a lot too."

Heidi smiled. She like the word important. She said, "I'm the oldest, aren't I?"

"Yep."

"It's okay, Heidi. Come see Mommy."

Heidi let go of Grandpa Glade's hand and ran to the bed. The bright morning sun made Mommy feel warm.

"How's my big girl?"

"I'm fine," said Heidi. Mommy looked the way she did when she was sick in bed, but she sounded like she always did. "Did the baby bring good stuff?"

"What?" Mommy looked at Grampa Glade.

He shrugged. "Who knows where these kids get things these days."

"Well, actually," said Mommy. "We have a surprise for you."

"What?"

"We have two babies."

"Two babies?"

"Yes."

"Twins?"

"Yes, a boy and a girl."

Heidi looked at Grampa Glade. "I'm doubly important!"

Mommy looked at him with a questioning looked. He grinned his elfish grin and shrugged.

Daddy walked into the room carry two little bundles, one pink and one blue. He knelt down by Heidi.

"Heidi," he said. "I like you to meet your brother and sister."

"What are their names?"

"We thought you would like to help."

"Can they be Christmas names?"

Daddy cringed a little and looked at Mommy and she said, "What do you have in mind?"

"We can name him Christmas."

Daddy blinked. "How about Christopher?

"Yeah, that's a real name, and it sounds like Christmas," said Heidi "He's like a present at Christmas."

"And her?

Heidi thought a moment. "She brought good stuff too." She looked at her Mommy, then her Daddy, then at Grampa Glade. The three adults leaned forward.

Heidi leaned to her sister and kissed her forehead. "Grace."

# WE THREE THUGS

So, we were casing out the store. I had "Zeke" on look out at the door, and Nic was over by the snack rack and frozen cola machine. Us Thugs were…

*Excuse me… Yeah, that's what we call ourselves...No, we aren't a gang….uh, we are like the Three Musketeers. It's just that we wanted something more up to date and tough. Something no one went by. Yeah, Ambrose came up with that. He's always reading and telling me to read more…. Ambrose? Oh, that's Zeke. He wanted a tougher sounding name than Ambrose, so we called him Zeke. The three of us formed a group, The Thugs. I'm the leader since I have been around more, foster homes and stuff. Ambrose and Nic kind of look up to me, and…anyway, I should get back to the story.*

Ambrose, I mean, "Zeke," was at the door, and, as I said, Nic was over by the frozen cola machine. I was down the aisle by the magazines, looking things over. Everything was cool. Ambrose gave me a nod. Someone was coming in. Nic coughed, the wait sign.

*What? No, we weren't really going to steal anything. Ambrose and Nic get bored, so I come up with these…uh…adventures for something to do. You see, they really have a dull life, so we…pretend. That was the last interruption, right?*

I was by the magazines. From behind me an army guy and his wife were moving down the aisle. They had one of those small plastic baskets with groceries: a small thing of milk, some bread and stuff. The guy was wearing a green camouflage jacket. He had short hair, but it was a little scraggly. The woman was young too. Dark hair and eyes. Real pretty. Really nice eyes. Especially compared to his. His looked a little angry. His forehead was all lines and stuff.

He was looking into his wallet and bumped into me. He gave me an eye. She whispered something like "Sorry." His eyes calmed down, and he says, "Yeah, sorry kid."

"No problem," I said.

She smiled at me. "Merry Christmas." Her smile was like lights on a tree, all bright.

"No problem," I say again. My cheeks felt warm.

They moved down the aisle. I heard her saying to him. "It's alright. Once we get …" she faded out. He had her arm around her now, and he was all looking about. His eyes watching "Zeke," Nic, and the clerk guy behind the counter. He seemed paranoid. That's when I noticed that she's pregnant. Then there's sound at the door, and his eyes shot around. Someone came in.

Amb…Zeke was giving me bug eyes. *Dude!* I had missed the signal that someone was coming. I shrugged and gave Nic a head nod toward the door. He nods. We were going to make ourselves gone.

See, the guy that came in the door was all jittery. He had wiry hair and was pale. Being that I was the only one of the three of us that really knew anything, I knew he was bad news. I had seen this guy in the streets, a druggie. His name was Harold. Thugs know when to avoid trouble.

But we did not avoid it soon enough.

Harold pulled a gun.

No one notices except me. Ambrose was by him and didn't even notice. Nic was walking by the army guy and his wife, who were at the counter with the clerk, some big guy with tattoos. He was smiling at the wife but keeping an eye on him.

Harold yelled, "Hey!" And everyone woke up.

Ambrose's eyes were huge, and he was frozen to the spot.

The clerk yelled too, reached under the counter and pulled out another gun.

The Army guy turned toward Harold and, with one arm, put his wife behind him. And with his other arm, and not even looking, he grabbed Nic and pushed him behind. He said, "Get down." He's all calm, yet I heard him say it through the yelling. Then she grabbed Nic and pulled him down by the counter and hugged him, keeping him away from everything.

And I stood there just like a plastic Santa in front of the store.

I couldn't make sense of the yelling, but then I got scared. Harold grabbed Ambrose and crouched behind him. He started shuffling toward the counter. The army guy was talking calmly to the clerk who started to lower his gun.

"No one needs to get hurt," he said. He lowered his one arm. I could read the name "Joseph" on his jacket.

"Right-oh, Soldier Boy," said Harold. "All I want is cash." His gun was shaking and awfully close to Ambrose's head.

Joseph nodded to the clerk. "Okay, now give him the money in the drawer."

He started to move, and then Harold said, "Hurry up, Fattie."

The clerk swore and pulled up his gun. Harold jerked up his gun up too. Then Joseph, just decks the clerk. And then he did this spin move and caught Harold on the nose. His head rocked back, and his arms went up in the air. The gun went off. That's when I hit the ground.

When I looked up, Joseph was breathing hard and looking about. His eyes were mad again. His wife was holding Nic and Ambrose. She was speaking to him. "It's all right," she said. "He's gone."

He looked at his wife, then the gun. His eyes were watery. He slowly set the gun on the counter.

"You okay?" he said.

She nodded. "Yes."

He held his hand out to her. She took it and got up. He looked down at Nic and Ambrose. "You boys okay?"

I heard them say "Yeah."

He looked at me. So did his wife. "You okay?"

That's when we heard the sirens. He looked about, thinking. He looked at the gun, started to reach for it, then stopped. He says to his wife, "Let's go." And they headed out the door, eyes down.

I got up and ran to Nic and Ambrose.

When I got to the counter, the clerk was standing up, swearing. "He took the money. They both took the money." I saw that the register was open.

Nic and Ambrose jumped up.

"Let's go."

And we ran.

Ambrose, Nic and I ran for a long time. We ran all the way back to the schoolyard, and that's when we saw that it was getting dark. Time to go home. Ambrose was still scared. He was crying. I told him to toughen up.

"Yeah," he said. "Okay."

Nic said, "Should we tell someone?"

"It's all done now," I said. "Not too much to say. Besides, the cops will get them both."

"He didn't do it," said Nic.

"What?"

"When the gun went off, the soldier was all weird-ed out. He was talking all kinds of stuff. Like he was under attack."

"Yeah," Ambrose jumped in. "He was calling for someone too."

Nic nodded. "He's calling for a chopper to come in. 'Man down.' 'Need a medic.'"

"And the robber guy was watching with blood running down his face. Then he sees the cash drawer open and grabs money and runs," said Ambrose.

"And then his wife starts talking to him. She grabs Ambrose and pulls him to the floor."

Ambrose nods. "She says he won't hurt us."

"Something about the war," said Nic.

"She says he's confused," said Ambrose.

"So, he's mental," I said.

Ambrose stepped up to me. "Don't say that." Ambrose never stepped up to me before. Ambrose's eyes were really close, and I could see the freckles on the bridge of his nose.

"Alright." I said. "Sorry, man." I bumped Ambrose with my chest to get him to back off. He stepped back. Ambrose had scared me. *Don't tell him, though.*

Anyway, Nic and Ambrose had to head for home. They had a place to be. I did too, but not so much as they did.

So, the next day, after school, I was just walking around downtown.

Ambrose and Nic had other things. And that's when I found myself down by Bethel Street by the pawnshops. I walked in the red one with the painted words when I see Joseph. He was in the store selling his tool belt; the kind carpenters wear. It had a hammer, measuring tape and some screwdrivers.

I ducked behind some shelves.

He said that he had a job going, and that he would be back next week. The guy was like, "Yeah. Sure." Joseph said it was over on Tower Hill, near Federal. He had a place over there, but he just lost his wallet and needed to make it to next week.

"Yeah," said the guy. "Sure."

Joseph, then said, "Don't let my wife know I was here. She'd be upset."

The guy behind the counter sighs. "Yeah, man. Your secret's safe."

"I'll be back," he said and went out the door.

I sat back a minute. Then, I headed out the door the other way and ducked into the alley.

Later, I told Ambrose and Nic what I had seen. That's when Nic told me he has Joseph's wallet.

"What?" I said.

"I have his wallet," Nic said again. "When he spun around and whacked Harold in the nose, it fell on the floor. I saw it after they left."

"And you grabbed it?"

"Yeah. When we were running out of there. I didn't want them to find it."

"He had to sell his tools so they could have money," I said.

"I still have it," said Nic.

"We need to give it back to him," said Ambrose.

"He's way over to the west," I said. "That's a long walk."

"Where?" said Ambrose. "I am going to take it back to him."

"You're nuts," I said.

"He needs his money."

"Nic," I said. "Finder keepers. Losers weepers. You just get rid of the wallet and use the money. We can get some good stuff with it."

"What?" His eyes were big.

"How much is there?"

"I didn't count it." Nic fidgeted. "Not much though."

Ambrose stepped between us. "We can't keep it," he said.

Nic looked at him, back at me, then him again. "Okay."

"You two are stupid." My face felt hot, and I clenched my fists.

"I am taking him his wallet," said Ambrose. His jaw was set, just like the other day.

"Me too," said Nic.

"Harold's out there." They both went pale and looked at each other.

"Yeah, so?" said Ambrose. His voice was a little shaky.

"We're not afraid," said Nic.

I knew they were. They hung out with me because I let them. They were kids with a mom and dad and regular meals. I was the tough one in the group. They wouldn't make it without me.

"To heck with you guys." I left.

So, it's after dark. I was not being missed at my so-called home, but I knew they would be. So I waited outside Ambrose's house. He snuck out the back window near eleven o'clock. He had a bag over his shoulder. It looked a bit heavy. He had what looked to be a flashlight in his hand; leave it to Ambrose to be prepared.

A few blocks over, he met up with Nic under a streetlight. I shook my head. Hadn't these guys learned anything from me? They weren't sticking to the shadows. Nic showed Ambrose the wallet. I groaned. *Not in public, you idiots.*

Then they headed west. I followed. I knew they wouldn't make it without me, so I had to keep an eye on them.

It had been an hour in the cold night. We were going through the grubby section of streets with broken windows, and that's when Harold found us.

I should say, when he found me and put me to a wall.

"Hey, kid."

"Let me go."

"I saw you at the store the other day, didn't I?" He was up in my face. His nose was bent and bruised, all dark and purple, even under the eyes. "I'm looking for Soldier Boy. You know where he is?

"How would I know?" I said. My voice was hoarse.

"You talk to any police?"

"Heck no," I said. "I ain't no narc."

"You sure you haven't seen Soldier Boy, anywhere?" He tilted his head for me to get a better look at his nose. "I have to return the favor."

"No," I said.

"Not at all."

"I haven't seen him."

"I'll have to go ask your buddies, I guess."

"Leave them alone," I said.

"Stick up for you buddies, eh?" He smiled all toothy. "Why are you following them?

"Just leave them alone. They don't know nuthin'."

"They know nuthin' about what?"

"Nothing about anything. They're stupid," I said. "They're just being stupid."

"You aren't though," he said. "You a survivor, like me?"

I had to bite my tongue. I was nothing like him, nor would I be.

"We got to stick together, guys like us."

"Yeah," I said.

"Okay, you keep quiet." He pressed me against the wall. "And I will go talk to your buddies."

I just got real mad, and with all I could, I kicked him in the groin. He sank low but had not let go of me. Not until a board hit him in the head. His eyes closed, and he fell to the ground. Ambrose and Nic stood side by side. Nic held a piece of wood in his hand. Ambrose had his plastic light saber glowing blue.

None of us said a word. Ambrose turned off his light saber and closed it up.

"Thugs," I said.

Thugs," they said, and we headed west.

We found the intersection of Tower Hill and Federal easy enough, but all about was houses galore.

"Look," said Nic. He pointed down the road to a large light shining down on the entrance to a construction site. Bethlehem Arms said the sign. "New affordable homes for families."

"That's where we go," said Ambrose.

"How in the world do you know?"

He looked at me. "You should read more," he said. "It's called symbolism."

"Plus," said Nic, "that's Joseph ducking between the fence and the bushes."

I looked at Ambrose who grinned. "Couldn't resist."

"Let's go," I said.

"But you should really read more," said Ambrose.

We followed Joseph's tracks back through the new neighborhood to the other side where the fence butts up against the shed of an animal clinic and its housing pens. Light shone through an opening. Ambrose and Nic were a little scared, so I pushed the panel aside and stepped through.

In a stall right in front of us was Joseph. He was kneeling by his wife. She was holding a little baby. Nic and Ambrose stepped in behind me. That's when Joseph stood up. He was beside her, ready to protect her and the baby, but he only saw us three kids.

"Hey," I said.

"Hey," he said.

"These are the boys from the store," said the new mom.

Joseph nods. "Yeah, Mary. I thought I recognized them."

"We have something you left." I glanced at Nic. He stepped forward and held out the wallet. "You dropped this," he said.

The wallet was packed with money, gobs of it. I'd bet anything that Nic had put his baseball money in the wallet.

Joseph took it. "I don't remember it being this full."

"Beats me." Nic grinned. "Things just happen."

"Thank you," said Mary. "But, we…"

Ambrose stepped forward. "I figured you need these too." He handed Joseph the bag.

When he opened it, his eyes got misty, and his jaw bunched up.

"What is it?" asked Mary.

He pulled his tool belt from the bag.

My jaw dropped. I wondered how and when Ambrose had gotten to the pawnshop. I decided Ambrose was one tough kid, name and all. *And I mean that.*

Joseph hung his head down, overwhelmed.

Mary smiled quietly and spoke to the baby, "And how did he get those?"

Joseph's eyes were wet. He looked at me, then Ambrose. Ambrose stood really tall. When he looked at Nic, he smiled and said, "Things just happen."

Laughter went around the barn.

It was then, I realized, I had nothing for any of them. I had no gift. No one said anything about it, either.

So, I did the one thing I never thought I would do. I sang. I was in a choir a few homes ago. Never told Ambrose or Nic 'cause they did not need to know. But, now, it was all I had.

"Silent night. Holy night…"

I was not even sure if I was singing it right. It had been awhile. Plus, I had to keep my eyes up high, so I couldn't see Ambrose and Nic's faces. I was afraid to look at them. By "So Holy and mild," they had joined in. On the second verse, Joseph and Mary sang too.

That's when the police opened the front door to the barn. But they did not yell or rush in, they waited. Apparently, they had been patrolling around because another unit had found Harold, and he had said that some kids beat him up.

There were questions and a lot of shuffling about. The older officer scratched his head a lot as we sat on bale of hay and told them the whole thing from the robbery on. Ambrose and Nic sat right next to me the whole time.

The other officer, King, talked to Joseph and Mary and then came over to us.

"What do you think, Sarge?" she asked, after the two talked quietly for a moment.

His radioed buzzed, and he answered. "Go ahead," he said.

"Hey, the Harold guy we picked up is wanted for that robbery a couple days ago."

"Looks like Christmas has done it's magic," he said.

"Yeah," said the voice on the radio. "He's all worked up though. And wants to press charges against the kids that beat him up."

"Really?"

"Yeah. Did you find any kids?"

The sergeant looked at Officer King. She seemed to shake her head.

"That's a negative," he said. "All the good kids are home in their beds." He turned his radio down. "Officer King, get these good kids home to bed."

We were shocked.

"What's going to happen to them?" I asked. We all three stood up.

Officer King smiled. "The Joseph's are a lucky family. The animal doctor, Doctor Shepherd, is a Veteran too. He's on his way to take the family to a home."

Everything blurred for a moment. We high-fived and danced and cheered. A moment later, we found Joseph on one knee in front us. Mary, holding the baby, was standing next to him.

"Hey, boys," he said. "Thank you for everything." His eyes were calm, at peace with the world. "You've have given us much tonight." He looked at Mary and back to us.

"What are your names?" said Mary.

"Nic."

"Ambrose."

"Max," I said. "The Thugs."

Mary, leaned forward, and ever so gently, said each of our names, and kissed us on the forehead. When she was done, she looked and smiled at the baby and her husband and at us and said, "We know four brave heroes."

Joseph stood with tears in his eyes. I glanced at the other two, they were crying. *Big babies.*

No matter, so was I.

*Yeah. We three Thugs.*

www.ingramcontent.com/pod-product-compliance
Lightning Source LLC
LaVergne TN
LVHW040925150826
845672LV00007B/2200

*9798756069938*